Will Smith

Julia Holt

Published in association with The Basic Skills Agency

Hodder & Stoughton
A MEMBER OF THE HODDER HEADLINE GROUP

The format details for this book are;
Arial, Normal 18, Single Spacing

Cover: Melinda Sue Gordon
Photos: Associated press; Corbis;
Ronald Grant Archive; Rex Features.

ISBN 034074734X

First published 1999
Year 2004 2003 2002

licences (for reprographic reproduction) may be obtained from the Copyright Licensing Agency Limited, of Tottenham Court Road, London W1P 9HE.

National Blind Children's Society
CustomEyes Books
Bradbury House
33 Market Street
Highbridge
Somerset
TA9 3BW

www.nbcs.org.uk

Registered Charity 1051607. A
Company Limited by guarantee.
Registered in England & Wales No.
3133018. Vat No. 879717554.

National Blind Children's Society has been helping visually impaired children and their families since 1995.

The Charity is unique in its focus on young people who face different challenges as they grow up. National Blind Children's Society is special in that it offers solutions, tailored to individual needs.

Technological developments create possible new learning experiences for the visually impaired, but too often these life-changing aids are beyond the financial reach of many families. National Blind Children's Society provides a vital service, ensuring through the supply of specially adapted computers, large print books, advocacy and grants that children receive the help they really need.

If you would like to help National Blind Children's Society in any way at all, please contact our offices on 01278 764764. We look forward to your call.

Contents

How many people do you know, who have starred in a sitcom based on their own life?

That's exactly what happened to Will Smith in 1989.

The sitcom was called The Fresh Prince of Bel Air and Will Smith was the star.

1 Childhood

Will was born on 25 September 1968 in Philadelphia, America.
He was named Willard Smith II after his father.

His father was an engineer and worked for schools.
They lived in a middle-class area with their four children.

Will was their second child.

He grew into a 6' 2" charmer.
He was very popular at school.

His teachers nicknamed him 'Prince' because he was always charming his way out of trouble.

Will did very well at school.

He won a place at university but he turned it down.

He wanted to try to make a career in showbusiness.

2 The Fresh Prince

Will started to call himself 'The Fresh Prince' when he teamed up with his friend Jeff at a party.

They started making rap music together.

They called themselves DJ Jazzy Jeff and the Fresh Prince.

Will Smith and DJ Jazzy Jeff at the
Grammy Awards.

Their music was called 'bubble gum
rap' because it was light and they
were not hard men.
But they were popular.

DJ Jazzy Jeff and The Fresh Prince became MTV stars.

They won Grammy awards in 1988 with the album 'He's The DJ, I'm The Rapper'.

They soon started to make lots of money.
They had hit singles like 'Parents Just Don't Understand'.
The clever words made US teenagers laugh.

Will made and spent a lot of money.

He had a house and cars and more jewellery than he could wear.

He was a millionaire at the age of 18.

His life was crazy in those days and in the end he owed a lot of money to the tax man.

When he was 21 Will was told of an idea.
The idea was to make a sitcom based on his life in Beverly Hills.

The life of a teenage millionaire and all the problems that could happen.

He decided to give it a go.
He was already famous as a rap star - now he could be famous as a TV star, with his own sitcom.

Will acted in his own sitcom, 'The Fresh Prince of Bel-Air'.

It was called 'The Fresh Prince of Bel Air'.

Will played the hero - a street-smart Philly kid who moves to Beverly Hills. He charms his way out of trouble just like Will.

It ran for six years and it helped Will to pay off the tax man.

In 1992 Will's son was born.

Will and his first wife, Sheree, called the baby Willard Smith III.
They nicknamed him Trey.

But Will and Sheree were not happy together.

The marriage did not work out.

When they divorced in 1995, Sheree got custody of Trey.

3 The Big Screen

While he was still working on the sitcom, Will took back his real name. In 1993 he moved from television onto the big screen.

In his first film he took the part of a gay con man who charms his way into a rich home.

Will proved he could act in the dramatic film 'Six Degrees Of Separation'.

'Bad Boys' was Will's first action film.

Will's next film in 1995 was the start of his career as an action hero.

The film was Bad Boys and it was a smash hit.

Now he could ask for $5 million for his next part and he got a lot of offers.

Will played a fighter pilot in
'Independence Day'.

4 Blockbusters

In 1996, Will chose a star part in a sci-fi blockbuster.
The film was called 'Independence Day'.

Will plays a wise-cracking fighter pilot called Captain Steve Hiller.

He defends the USA by fighting off an alien attack.

'Independence Day' made more money than any other film in 1996.

A year later Will made another sci-fi film.
Men In Black is a sci-fi comedy.

This time he plays Jay, a wise-cracking federal agent.

He wears a black suit and dark sunglasses.

He has to save the whole planet from alien attack.

The film was a huge success and made a lot of money.

In the film 'Men In Black'.

In the same year as 'Men In Black' Will also went back to making rap music.

He made the album 'Big Willie Style'. It is his first album without DJ Jazzy Jeff.

Will also had a huge hit with the song 'Men In Black', which was the theme song from the film.

Will Smith does not look like the kind of actor who plays action hero parts.

He says that he could play Dumbo the elephant because he has big ears.

But his quick wit gives him his own place among the action heroes.

It is no surprise that his own hero is the comedian and film star, Eddie Murphy.
Will and Jada were married on the last day of 1997.

At the end of 2000 Will and Jada had a baby girl.
They called her Willow.

Jada says that Will is learning every single day, how to be a good father.

He's in demand for more films and he has a new record deal.

You can envy Will's success.
But it is impossible not to like him.

Will with some of this fans.

Will kept his two careers going in 1998.
He starred in a thriller called 'Enemy of the State'.
In the film, Will played a man on the run from the CIA.

He also had two hits in the UK, with 'Just The Two Of Us' and 'Miami'.

In 1999 Will's success was mixed.
His film 'Wild Wild West' did not make its costs back.
But the theme song was a big hit.

Then, at the end of the millennium Will's new album came out.
He was very cheeky.
He called it Willennium.
It was a huge hit.

Will and Jada.

Will spent the next year in training for
a big film.
He had to get very fit to star as
Muhammad Ali.

The film was called 'Ali'.
It came out in 2001 It was the story of
a legend.
Ali – the boxer and the man.

After 'Ali', Will went on to play Agent J
again in Men in Black 2.
The worm aliens are back again, but
this time they are led by a woman.
The film will be out in 2002.

5 President Will?

Will was asked what he was going to do next.
He said: 'I want to do everything.
I want to be the first black president.
Give me ten years.'

He will not be the first actor to become president.

Ex-president Ronald Reagan used to be a film star.

So look out for President Will Smith in the next few years.

33

Will Smith plays a fighter pilot in 'Independence Day' – but could he defend America for real as President of the USA?